To Lorraine,

and many thanks,
Barbara Beard

LAMMIE PIE, PRIVATE EYE

BARBARA BEARD

AuthorHouse™
1663 Liberty Drive
Bloomington, IN 47403
www.authorhouse.com
Phone: 1 (800) 839-8640

Published by AuthorHouse 08/21/17

ISBN: 978-1-5462-0510-4 (sc)
ISBN: 978-1-5462-0509-8 (e)
ISBN: 978-1-5462-0511-1 (hc)

Library of Congress Control Number: 2017912998

Print information available on the last page.

Any people depicted in stock imagery provided by Thinkstock are models,
and such images are being used for illustrative purposes only.
Certain stock imagery © *Thinkstock.*

This book is printed on acid-free paper.

Because of the dynamic nature of the Internet, any web addresses or links contained in this book may have changed
since publication and may no longer be valid. The views expressed in this work are solely those of the author and do not
necessarily reflect the views of the publisher, and the publisher hereby disclaims any responsibility for them.

authorHOUSE®

On the top of a mountain
In a land way up high
Lived a little brown dog
Lammie Pie, Private Eye

She was soft and cuddly
Brown and curly and kind
Constant friend and companion
The best you could find

Now Lammie had powers
She was clever and keen
She could sniff out the answer
To problems not seen

She could sense there was danger
Down below or up high
With her nose to the ground
And her tail to the sky

She would snuffle and sniff
Dig and grovel and search
Never stopping 'til finding
The dangers that lurked

And that danger was present!
Her friend Sammie came pleading
To find his lost smile
That he surely was needing

Don't worry, said Lammie
I'm quick witted and cunning,
Did it fall off while walking
Or while you were running?

Just as I was running
Back here from the stable
I was visiting the horses
My favorite is Mable..

Well that's fine and good,
I'm sure Mable's a beauty
Now you've lost your smile
And to find it's my duty!

She grabbed her spyglass
Her pencil and paper
The OFFICIAL CLUE BOOK
To help solve this smile caper!

She turned and said "Sammie
please know that I'm able
My plan is to have
A chat with horse Mable."

Lammie Pie, Private Eye
Was soon out of view
She'd solve this case quickly
Smartest dog you ever knew.

Down at the barnyard
Lammie found Mable
She was having her lunch
At a cute corner table

"Hi Mable," said Lammie
"I'm here on a case
You know Sammie is missing
The smile from his face!"

"Oh, dear," uttered Mable
"Not his beautiful smile!
He had it on earlier,
Down that road 'bout a mile"

"I thank you, horse Mable,
I'll follow your hunch
And thanks for your time,
Now back to your lunch!"

12

Down that dusty dirt road
Lammie trotted with haste
To see if Sam's smile
Was there, just in case.

And sure enough Lammie
Looked there on the ground
with her official spyglass
Sammie's big smile was found!

Whew! That was lucky!
Sammie's steps we retraced
And found that big smile
That belongs on his face

Oh Sam he was grateful
His smile was ok!
And thinking hard he remembered
What had happened that day

Sammie said "Ah yes,
I'm embarrassed to say
A cat was chasing me
I had to run away!"

"I was running so fast
From this cat big and brown
That my smile fell right off
Replaced by a frown!"

"I just kept on going
I ran faster and faster,
and when I looked back
I was very much past her!"

"Wow", exclaimed Lammie
What courage you've shown!
By far you're the bravest
Dog I've ever known!"

"And now you're all better
Don't worry with that
And I promise I won't say
You were chased by a CAT!"

So remember if ever
Your smile's lost and you cry
Just call on your friend
Lammie Pie, Private Eye

.....With her nose to the ground
and her tail to the sky
if you want to know why
just ask.......Lammie Pie, Private Eye

CPSIA information can be obtained
at www.ICGtesting.com
Printed in the USA
BVOW05*0232100917

494396BV00007B/17/P